NORTHERN BEACHES
SYDNEY • AUSTRALIA

This book is dedicated to my best friend, Jesus.

KEN DUNCAN
PANOGRAPHS®

INTRODUCTION

For John & Margaret
Hope you will come visit in Sydney soon

Sydney's Northern Beaches is an area which has special meaning for me, as the years I spent there had a great influence on my life.

So many familiar places, yet while shooting this book I was forced to look again with new purpose. In the course of our busy lives, it is easy for beauty to escape our attention. Hurrying to work or school or the shopping, even those who live in a paradise like the one revealed in these pages can overlook their surroundings.

The Northern Beaches is a major jewel in Sydney's crown and I'm glad to share with you a place which is so close to my heart.

TITLE PAGE
Surf check, Collaroy Beach

THIS PAGE
Barrenjoey Lighthouse, Palm Beach

NEXT PAGE
Manly Beach

I would like to offer my sincere thanks to the sponsors who have endorsed this project. It is only with their support and assistance that we have been able to produce this book.

MANLY PACIFIC PARKROYAL

So close to Sydney, yet with all the beauty of the peninsula on your doorstep, is the relaxed, cosmopolitan resort atmosphere of Manly and the international standard of the Manly Pacific Parkroyal. Telephone: (02) 9977 7666.

WARRIEWOOD SQUARE

Situated in Jackson's Road Warriewood, in the heart of the Northern Beaches, offering customers a relaxed shopping environment, with Kmart, Coles, Franklins and over 65 speciality stores.

NATIONWIDE REALTY PARKER ROBSON

Our company endeavours to consistently achieve the highest standard of service and professionalism, and aspires to being the best in our field. Telephone: (02) 9948 0291.

NORTHERN BEACHES WEEKENDER

The peninsula's own newspaper, providing news, information and entertainment for all sectors of the community. Telephone: (02) 9905 7888.

PREVIOUS PAGE
*Upper Gledhill Falls,
Ku-ring-gai Chase National Park*

THIS PAGE
Curl Curl Beach Rock Pool

NEXT PAGE
Aerial view of Palm Beach

DOGS
PROHIBITED

Sydney is a city where land and water are interlocked as intricately as the pieces in a jigsaw puzzle, and nowhere can this be seen more clearly than on the Northern Beaches, where every house lies within sight - or within the smell - of the sea.

PREVIOUS PAGE
Sunrise, North Curl Curl Beach

THIS PAGE
Pathway to Mona Vale Beach

NEXT PAGE
Aerial view of Long Reef

PREVIOUS PAGE
Picnic on Store Beach

THIS PAGE
Turimetta Beach

A stormy day, Barrenjoey Head

A new day, Barrenjoey Head

Clear sky and stinging sunshine, inviting these colourful crowds into the gleaming, cool water. Their shrieking excitement fills the air. Three children, with innocent intentness, have laboured happily for a length of time they have not noticed passing, creating a castle large enough to sit in as though it were an armchair. In their concentration, they have not realised that the tide is rising - now their creation has been swamped.

This scene confirmed to me that none of life's pleasures last forever; only God's peace within is eternal.

PREVIOUS PAGE
Aerial view of Scotland Island

THIS PAGE
Swamped by a wave, Avalon Beach

NEXT PAGE
Ambitious swimmers, Newport Baths

PREVIOUS PAGE
America Bay Walk, Ku-ring-gai Chase National Park

THIS PAGE
Palm Beach Wharf, Pittwater

NEXT PAGE
Sunrise, Avalon Beach

PREVIOUS PAGE
The Spit - gateway to the Northern Beaches

THIS PAGE
Sandstone cliffs

NEXT PAGE
Aerial view of Whale Beach

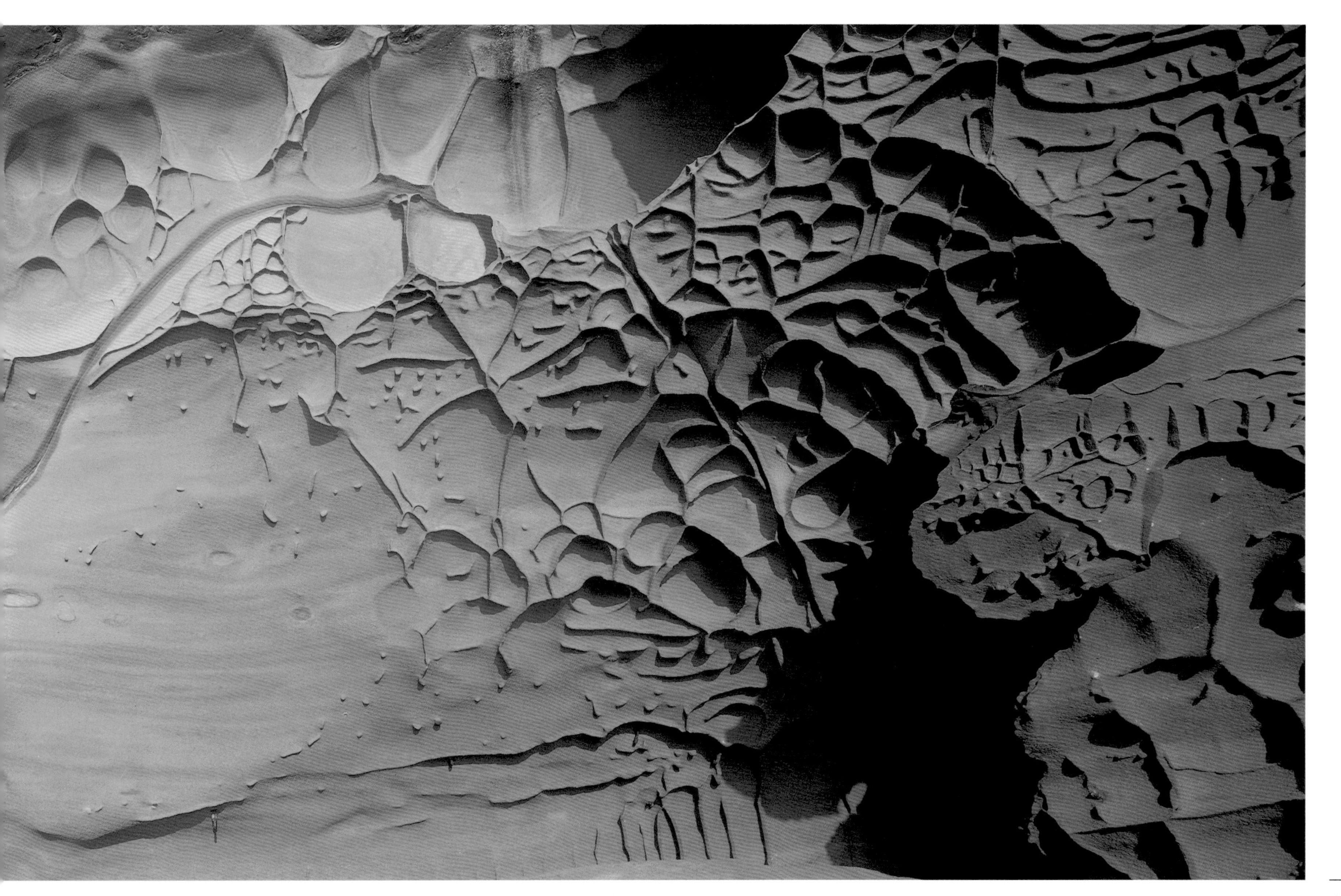

Sunrise, looking north, Manly Beach

Sunrise, looking south, Manly Beach

EVINRUDE 35
YAMAHA

Humble aluminium dinghies, tethered to a wooden jetty. Who could guess that such an unassuming scene is the gateway to another world, and a unique lifestyle? For the inhabitants of Scotland Island, this wharf is a vital link to the outside world, both for supplies and services, and for the work most of them travel to during the day.

The island is a haven to which they escape from the pressures of modern life. Yet like other forms of paradise, it is not easily attained: on the coldest winter mornings, the journey to work in these small open boats would not be envied by those who ride in the air-conditioned comfort of cars.

PREVIOUS PAGE
High tide, Newport Beach

THIS PAGE
Commuter Wharf, Church Point

PREVIOUS PAGE
Upper Gledhill Falls in flood, Kur-ring-gai Chase National Park

THIS PAGE
Freshwater Beach at sunrise

NEXT PAGE
Aerial view of Dee Why

PREVIOUS PAGE
Basking in the sun, Manly Beach

THIS PAGE
Mona Vale Beach

NEXT PAGE
Boats at Bayview

Clear waters, Palm Beach

THIS PAGE
Surfer girl, Palm Beach

NEXT PAGE
Barrenjoey Head

ARMSTRONGS

PREVIOUS PAGE
Shelly Beach, Cabbage Tree Bay

THIS PAGE
Manly Wharf

NEXT PAGE
Sunrise, Turimetta Beach

A stormy day. Warm and safe in my beachside cottage, I listen to waves which break like thunderclaps, ghostly howling wind, the rush of rain. It would seem foolish to venture outside in such weather, but some urge beyond my understanding impels me to go.

Soon the rain begins to ease, and the clouds part as though a great stone had been rolled aside, opening a doorway of pure light. A solitary fisherman stands baiting his hook while the clouds continue to boil and stream around him, as though at the very moment of creation.

If we prefer the comfort of shelter, we can miss many such opportunities for revelation and adventure.

THIS PAGE
Fisherman, Mona Vale Pool

NEXT PAGE
Narrabeen Beach

WARNING
SLIPPERY SURFACE
ON POOL SURROUNDS
& ROCK SHELVES

PREVIOUS PAGE
Aerial view of Balgowlah Heights and Fairlight

THIS PAGE
Sunrise, North Whale Beach

THIS PAGE
Sunrise, Bilgola Beach

NEXT PAGE
Sunrise reflections, Bayview

Sunrise, Queenscliff Beach

NORTHERN BEACHES, SYDNEY AUSTRALIA
First published in 1996
by Ken Duncan Panographs® Pty Limited
ACN 050 235 606
P.O. Box 15, Wamberal NSW 2260, Australia. Telephone: (02) 4367 6777.
Reprinted 1997, 1998

Designed by Good Catch Design.
Edited by Jamie Grant.
Colour separations by Hi Rez Digital Imaging.
Printed by South China Printing Co. Hong Kong.

The National Library of Australia Cataloguing-in-Publication entry:
Duncan, Ken
Northern Beaches, Sydney Australia.
ISBN 0 9586681 0 8.
1. Beaches - New South Wales - Sydney - Pictorial works.
2. Sydney (N.S.W.) - Pictorial works. I. Title.
994.41